RUSSIA

David Cumming

CHERRYTREE BOOKS

LETTERS FROM AROUND THE WORLD

Titles in this series

AUSTRALIA · BANGLADESH · BRAZIL · CANADA · CHINA · COSTA RICA · EGYPT · FRANCE · GERMANY · GREECE · INDIA · INDONESIA · ITALY · JAMAICA · JAPAN · KENYA · MEXICO · NIGERIA · PAKISTAN · RUSSIA · SAUDI ARABIA · SOUTH AFRICA · SPAIN · SWEDEN · THE USA

A Cherrytree Book

Conceived and produced by

Nutshell
MEDIA

www.nutshellmedialtd.co.uk

VISIT OUR WEBSITE www.evansbooks.co.uk

First published in 2007 by
Evans Brothers Ltd
2A Portman Mansions
Chiltern Street
London W1U 6NR

© Copyright Evans Brothers 2007

Editor: Polly Goodman
Designer: Tim Mayer
Map artwork: Encompass Graphics Ltd
All other artwork: Tim Mayer

All photographs were taken by David Cumming. Page 21 is courtesy of Eye Ubiquitous/Hutchison/David Cumming.

Acknowledgements
The author would like to thank the following for their help with this book: Professor Euphym Vyshkin and his staff in the Department of Linguistics at Samara State University of Architecture and Civil Engineering, as well as Roman, Elena, Dennis and Elizaveta Vyshkin.

British Library Cataloguing in Publication Data
Cumming, David, 1953
   Letters from Russia. – (Letters from around the world)
   1. Russia (Federation) – Social life and customs –
   Juvenile literature
   I. Title
947'.086

ISBN-13: 9781842343784

Cover: Elizaveta with her best friends, Eugenia (left) and Svetlana (right).
Title page: Elizaveta, Eugenia and Svetlana in the playground behind Elizaveta's home.
This page: Forests (taiga) cover these hills in Siberia, eastern Russia.
Contents page: Elizaveta loves eating ice cream all year round, even in the middle of winter.
Glossary page: Elizaveta's class has an English lesson.
Further Information page: The Kremlin, in the centre of Moscow. This is where the people in charge of Russia work.
Index: Samara has been built alongside the River Volga, the longest river in Europe.

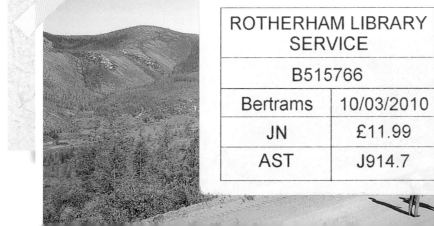

Contents

My Country

Tuesday, 3 February

PO Box 421
Samara
Russia 443001

Dear Chris,

Privet! (You say 'pree-VET'. This means 'Hi' in Russian.)

My name is Elizaveta Vyshkina (you say 'VISH-keena'). I'm 9 years old and I live in Samara, a city in Russia. I've got an older brother called Dennis, who is 16 years old. Do you have any brothers or sisters?

Here's some information for your class project on Russia. To show that you're female, in Russia your surname has an 'a' on the end. So I'm Miss Vyshkina, but Dennis is Mr Vyshkin.

From

Elizaveta

Here I am with my father Roman, my mother Elena and my brother Dennis.

Russia is a vast country that stretches from Europe across Asia. It used to be part of the USSR. This huge empire split up in 1991, when Russia became a separate country. Since then, life for most Russians has been very difficult.

Russia's place in the world.

Russia is by far the biggest country in the world. It is nearly the size of the USA and Canada joined together.

Samara is on the huge River Volga. During the Second World War (1939–45), Samara was the capital of Russia. The government and important industries moved to the city to escape the invading German army.

Today, Samara still has many industries, including making space rockets, chemicals and sweets. The city has good transport links, which help its industries run smoothly. Materials for the factories are brought by boat on the Volga, or by train.

This is the main shopping street in the old part of Samara. Most people travel around the city by bus, but an underground metro is also being built.

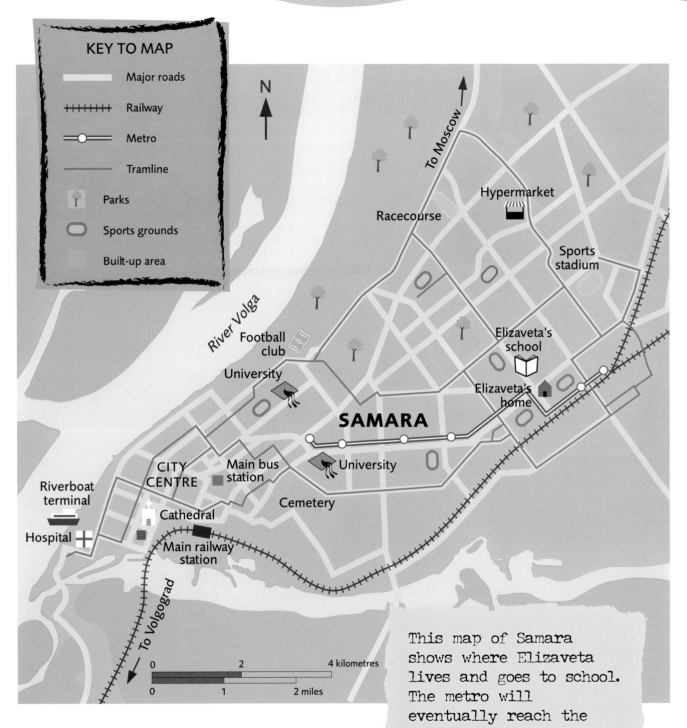

KEY TO MAP

Major roads

Railway

Metro

Tramline

Parks

Sports grounds

Built-up area

N

River Volga

To Moscow

Racecourse

Hypermarket

Sports stadium

Football club

University

Elizaveta's school

Elizaveta's home

SAMARA

University

Cemetery

CITY CENTRE

Main bus station

Riverboat terminal

Cathedral

Hospital

Main railway station

To Volgograd

0   2   4 kilometres

0   1   2 miles

This map of Samara shows where Elizaveta lives and goes to school. The metro will eventually reach the main railway station.

People in Samara are proud of their new main railway station, which is the tallest in Russia. The city is also a famous place for learning. Students come here from all over Russia to study at its universities and colleges.

Landscape and Weather

Russia has many different landscapes and climates. Much of the north is within the Arctic Circle. Here, temperatures can drop to −70°C in winter. There are thick forests, called taiga, across the middle of Russia.

In this town, in northern Siberia, enormous pipes carry hot water to heat homes during the very cold winters.

In the south, the land is almost desert because the summers are so hot and dry. In the east, there are active volcanoes on the Kamchatka Peninsula, which sticks out into the Pacific Ocean. Samara is surrounded by flat land, called steppe, which has good soils for farming. This area has hot summers and very cold winters, with little rain.

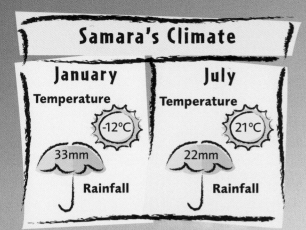

Samara's Climate

January

Temperature

-12°C

33mm

Rainfall

July

Temperature

21°C

22mm

Rainfall

In the summer in Samara, the River Volga is warm enough for swimming. In the winter it often freezes, with ice thick enough to drive cars on.

At Home

Like most children in Russia, Elizaveta lives in a flat. It's on the top floor of a five-storey building. The block is on one of the main streets in Samara, but the double-glazed windows help to keep the traffic noise out. The double-glazing also keeps out draughts, stopping the flat from getting cold in the winter.

Elizaveta's flat is on the top floor of this block of flats. It has a covered balcony.

Elizaveta and Dennis share a computer in their bedroom. They use it to do their homework and to play games.

It's a Russian custom to take off your shoes whenever you enter a home. It helps to keep the dirt out.

Elizaveta's flat has a narrow hallway, a lounge, two bedrooms, and a small kitchen and bathroom. Elizaveta shares one of the bedrooms with her brother Dennis. In Russia this is quite normal because most flats are small.

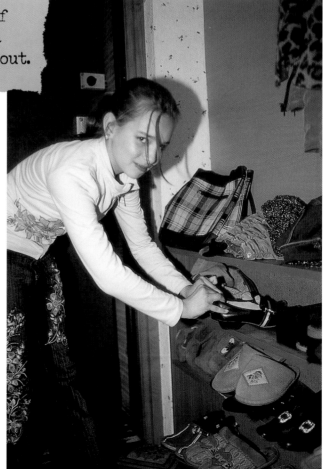

In the winter, hot water is pumped from Samara's power station to homes all around the city. The hot water fills the radiators and gives everyone central heating. With winter temperatures often dropping to −40°C, it is essential to have heating.

Wednesday, 9 March

PO Box 421
Samara
Russia 443001

Privet (Hi) Chris!

Thanks for your letter. Yes, you're right. Most Russians do own a dacha. That's what we call a country cottage where people go in the summer for the weekend and holidays. We don't have our own dacha, but my grandparents have one near Samara that we visit instead. We cook on a barbecue outside most nights — it's great! There's also a small swimming pool that we use when it's hot.

Write again soon.

Paka! (Bye!)

Elizaveta

This is the dacha near Samara where we go in the summer.

Food and Mealtimes

For breakfast, Elizaveta eats *blinis* (say 'bleenies'), which are small, round pancakes. Sometimes she also has a frankfurter sausage.

Another favourite is *vermicelli* (say 'verm-i-chelly'), which is like very thin spaghetti. Russians eat it for breakfast cooked in milk or with cheese on top. Elizaveta drinks tea, coffee or sometimes milk.

On this breakfast table, there are apples, tomatoes, eggs, sausages, cheese, roast beef, sour cream, cauliflower cheese and baked potatoes.

Elizaveta's mother buys all
her fruit and vegetables
daily at this market.

For lunch, Elizaveta usually has a bowl of soup
with bread. In winter, the soup is often *borscht*
(say 'borshh'), which is made from beetroots.
In summer it is *akroshka* (say 'ack-ROSH-kar'),
a cold soup made with
kvas (say 'kwass'),
vegetables and bits of
meat. It is flavoured
with chopped dill.

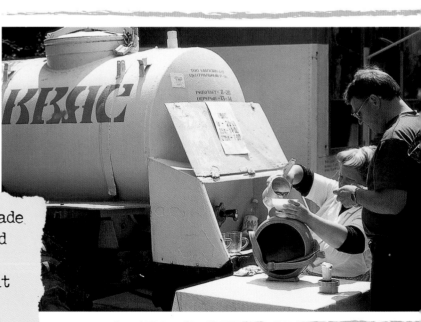

Kvas is a refreshing drink made
from sugar and rye. It is sold
from big containers on the
streets and can also be bought
in cans from shops.

For dinner, after finishing the *akroshka* soup, there is *pilaff*, *pilmeny*, deep-fried salmon parcels and salad to eat, followed by tea and cake.

In the evening, dinner consists of either *pilaff* (rice with vegetables and meat), *pilmeny* (dumplings stuffed with a mixture of chopped meat and vegetables), fried fish and vegetables, or meat and potatoes.

Like most Russians, Elizaveta likes ice cream, even in winter when there's snow on the ground.

Thursday, 17 June

PO Box 421
Samara
Russia 443001

Privet Chris!

Here's a delicious recipe for Russian salad, which we eat a lot during the summer. It's quick and easy to make, and very healthy.

You need: 120g cooked peas, 100g cooked beetroot, 120g cooked carrots, 100g boiled potatoes, 40g pickled vegetables (like cucumbers or gherkins), mayonnaise, chopped dill, pinch of salt and pepper

1. Cut the beetroot, carrots, potatoes and pickled vegetables into small cubes of the same size.
2. Put them in a bowl, along with the peas, and mix in enough mayonnaise to 'glue' them all together.
3. Add the salt and pepper, and decorate the salad with the dill.

Delicious!

From

Elizaveta

You can make your own version of Russian salad — just use your favourite vegetables and herbs instead of the ones mentioned in the recipe.

School Day

Like most of her friends, Elizaveta walks to school every day. It takes her about 15 minutes to get there. Classes begin at 8.30 a.m. and finish at 12.30 p.m. Each lesson lasts for 40 minutes.

There are 900 pupils in Elizaveta's school. Like most schools in Russia, it is run by the government. This means that it is free.

Like all city schools in Russia, Elizaveta's school does not have a name, just a number. Her school is number 65.

Here is Elizaveta with her class teacher, talking about a project Elizaveta is doing on famous Russian writers.

Like all government schools, Elizaveta's school is mixed (there are boys and girls) and there is no uniform.

Elizaveta studies maths, music, English, Russian language and literature, PE and art. Like most Russian schools, Elizaveta's school does not have much equipment because the government is short of money for things like computers and books.

Elizaveta's class is in the fourth year. They've been coming to school since the age of 6.

When school finishes at 12.30 p.m., Elizaveta goes home for lunch. She goes back to school in the afternoon for extra lessons in English and music. Her parents must pay a little for these classes.

The school has four terms a year, with three short holidays (in mid-November, early January and late March) and one long summer holiday.

Friday, 3 July

PO Box 421
Samara
Russia 443001

Privet Chris!

It's our summer holidays at the moment and we're just back from camp. We have summer camp in June every year, at the beginning of the summer holiday. The camp's organized by the school. Our parents, brothers and sisters can come, too. We stay in log cabins by the River Volga, not far from Samara. We do lots of team sports, go fishing, take part in nature rambles and have a lot of barbecues. It's great fun.

What do you do in your school holidays? Write back and tell me.

Paka! (Bye!)

Elizaveta

Here are some of my friends at summer camp. This year we put on a play with puppets.

Off to Work

Elizaveta's dad, Roman, teaches sport. Her mum, Elena, looks after the home. However, most other women in Russia have to work, to make enough money for their families.

Russia is rich in natural resources and many people are employed in industries connected with them, such as mining and forestry. The country makes a lot of money by selling oil, natural gas, metals and timber to other countries.

These tractors have been made using iron and steel from Russia.

Many people in Samara have to earn extra money by selling things from stalls on street pavements.

Before 1991, when Russia was part of the USSR, many factories were badly run. Since then, many have had to close and workers have found it hard to find new jobs.

This gold has been mined in Siberia. Russia has the world's largest amount of gold in the ground.

Free Time

Elizaveta loves sport, especially badminton. She practises twice a week and has done well in lots of competitions.

When she's not playing badminton, Elizaveta likes spending time with her friends, in the playground outside her flat, in the park nearby, or watching DVDs or videos.

Elizaveta trains with a Russian badminton champion and hopes to follow in her footsteps.

The success of Russia's Olympic team has made volleyball a popular sport all over the country. In the summer, it's played outdoors.

Monday, 31 August

PO Box 421
Samara
Russia 443001

Privet Chris!

Thanks for your letter. I like going to the movies, too. We get all the latest films over here, but they're not in English. Most Russians do not understand English, so all our films are in Russian. You would probably find it funny to hear someone like Tom Cruise speaking in Russian! Of course, it's not really him, just a Russian actor saying his lines.

What films have you seen recently?

From

Elizaveta

Here are posters for two films, written in Russian. One of the films stars Tom Cruise.

Religion and Festivals

When Russia was part of the USSR, religion was forbidden. Churches and all other places of worship were locked up or even knocked down.

Today, even though people are free to worship again, few Russians are interested in religion. Most Russians who are religious follow the Russian Orthodox faith. The next largest religion is Islam.

Russian Orthodox churches have dome-shaped roofs called onion domes, which are beautifully painted with special crosses on top.

This is a special open-air church service by the side of the River Volga.

Elizaveta lights a candle for luck in a Russian Orthodox church. All women must cover their heads in church.

The most important religious festival in the Russian Orthodox Church is Easter. On the Saturday evening before Easter Sunday, people go to church with *paskha* (a special cheesecake) and *kulich* (sweet bread) for the priest to bless. Christmas Day is on 8 January.

New Year (1 January) is the biggest non-religious holiday in Russia. Friends and families gather together on New Year's Eve and 'Grandfather Frost' brings presents for children.

Fact File

Capital city: Moscow, which is famous for its Red Square (above), where there is the Kremlin, the home of the government.

Other major cities: St. Petersburg, Novosibirsk, Yekaterinburg, Nizhniy Novgorod, Omsk.

Size: 17,075,200km². Russia is so large that it has 11 different time zones. As people in Moscow are going to bed, people on the Pacific coast are getting up the next day.

Population: 142,893,540.

Main religions: Russian Orthodox (75%), Islam (10%) and small numbers of Protestants, Jews and Buddhists.

Flag: Three equal, horizontal strips of white, blue and red.

Languages: Russian is spoken by 81% of the people. There are over 100 other languages, including Tartar, Ukrainian, Chuvash and Bashkir. Russian is the fourth most spoken language in the world.

Currency: The rouble, divided in kopeks (100 kopeks = 1 rouble).

Longest rivers: Yenisey (5,550km), Amur (4,410km), Lena (4,260km), Volga (3,685km). Although not the longest, the Volga is considered the most important river in Russia because it is used for transport, and for providing electricity and water for millions of people. The Volga is also the longest river in Europe, of which western Russia is a part.

Highest mountain: Mount Elbrus (5,642m).

Main industries: Oil, gas, metal production, chemicals, forestry.

Famous Russians: Yuri Gagarin (1934–68) was a cosmonaut who became the first person in space, in 1961. Anna Kournikova (born 1981) was a champion tennis player before she retired. Garry Kasparov (born 1963) is a champion chess player.

Main festivals: Easter, New Year, Russian Orthodox Christmas, Victory Day (9 May, which celebrates the defeat of Nazi Germany in 1939).

Deepest lake: Lake Baikal (1,637m) is also the world's deepest lake.

History: Over the centuries, the small region of Russia (near Moscow) expanded until it controlled a huge empire. This Russian Empire stretched from the edge of eastern Europe right across Asia to the Pacific Ocean. The empire was ruled by a royal family until 1917, when the Communist Party took charge of it. The communists renamed the empire the Union of Soviet Socialist Republics (USSR). In 1991, the USSR was split up and Russia became a country.

Stamps: Russian stamps show a variety of things, including history, sports and the military.

Glossary

capital The most important city in a country, which is not always the biggest.

climate The normal weather in a place.

dacha A Russian country cottage that is used mostly in the summer.

desert A large area of very dry, dusty land.

double-glazing A window with two panes of glass instead of one, which helps to keep noise and cold out.

government The group of people elected to run a country.

industry Making things in factories to sell.

kvas (say 'kwass') A traditional Russian summer drink made from sugar and rye flour, with a sweet-sour taste.

metro An underground railway system in a city.

natural resources The natural wealth of a country, such as coal and minerals.

peninsula A long area of land that is almost surrounded by water.

population The number of people who live in an area.

Russian Orthodox Church The Russian part of the Christian Church.

steppe A huge area of grassy, treeless land in eastern Europe and Asia.

tramline A line of rails that vehicles called trams run along, driven by electricity.

USSR The initials of the Union of Soviet Socialist Republics, the name given to the Russian Empire after 1917.

volcano A mountain with a hole in the top. It can erupt, throwing out lava and ash through the hole.

volleyball A game in which two teams hit a large ball over a net with their hands.

Further Information

Information books:

The Changing Face of Russia by Galya Ransome (Hodder, 2003)

Polina's Day by Andrey Ilyn (Frances Lincoln, 2005)

A World of Recipes: Russia by Sue Townsend (Heinemann, 2004)

Fiction:

The Kingfisher Book of Tales from Russia (Kingfisher, 2000)

Masha and the Firebird by Margaret Bateson-Hill (Zero to Ten, 2001)

Old Peter's Russian Tales by Arthur Ransome (Nissen Books, 2003)

Little Daughter of the Snow by Arthur Ransome (Frances Lincoln, 2005)

The Firebird and Other Russian Fairy Tales by Arthur Ransome (Dover, 2004)

Websites:

CIA World Factbook
www.cia.gov/cia/publications/factbook
Up-to-date facts and figures on Russia and other countries.

Super Russian Websites
www.uni.edu/becker/Russian2.html
A site with links to information about Russia, both past and present.

The Moscow Times
www.themoscowtimes.com/indexes/01.html
An English-language newspaper with all the latest news in Russia.

Way to Russia
www.waytorussia.net
A site for tourists, with lots of general information on Russia.

Index